Raising Sinners

Lisa Clark

Raising Sinners
by Lisa Clark

Printed in the United States of America.

ISBN 9781498474078

p. 61 Nancy Leigh DeMoss, *Lies Women Believe and the Truth that Sets them Free*; Moody Publishers, 2001

www.xulonpress.com

Contents

DISCLAIMER/ ACKNOWLEDGMENTS/ DEDICATIONS

Disclaimer: This is not a literary work of art. I'm not that smart.

Acknowledgments: Many, many thank yous to my *forever friends* who gave of their time and talents to edit this book. They read and reread this manuscript and helped me look like a decent author. They are so good. Thank you *Keena Pratt*, *Carrie Stockdale*, and *Cynthia Sanders*. You are precious to me. You were so tender and thoughtful with me and treated this like a labor of love, and I'm forever grateful and thankful to each of you.

Thank you to my dear friend, *Linda Paulk*, for writing the foreword to this book. Your friendship is pure gold. Your faith in me to help launch the SkyMoms Ministry in 2007 through Sky Ranch Christian Camps has forever changed my life. Thank you for the encouragement and for your partnership in ministry.

Dedications: My beloved, *BC*: You started this whole thing. It was you who gave me the confidence to step out and believe that I was able. You are it for me. It.

To my girls, *Caroline* and *Camryn*: Being your mom has been the biggest blessing in my life. You have lived lives that have given me lots of material, and you've chosen the less traveled path, which has given me the evidence necessary to continue encouraging moms that it is possible to raise sinners to love Jesus with their whole heart. I love you dearly.

To my sons-in-law, *Brent* and *Brett*: I don't even know what to say, really. My eyes are filling with tears as I write this. All I know to say is, God is good! You two guys far exceeded our expectations. We prayed for you. And God showed up and out big time. You are *the best*. Thank you for loving our girls like Christ loves His Church.

Foreword

R*aising Sinners* is a collection of material Lisa Clark has written from the lens of her own personal parenting experience. Moms will easily relate to her refreshing transparency as she captures the many emotions we all experience as moms. Lisa challenges us to embrace this parenting journey. Her book is a fun, fresh, relevant, and real compilation sure to stimulate a connection with you in your own personal parenting adventure.

In almost fifty-four years of life here on earth, it has become evident to me that God places people in our lives to provide friendship, accountability, honesty, prayers, and wise counsel. Are you with me? So thankful for this. Lisa Clark is one of these people in my life. Our divine connection and friendship has impacted my life personally and professionally in countless ways.

I first met Lisa at church twenty-five years ago when my husband and I moved our family and company to the Dallas area. Together, we raised children, played Keno, shared milestone birthdays, hosted baby and bridal showers, and for the last nine years have partnered in ministry to moms through Sky Ranch. Shortly after I accepted the call to serve at Sky Ranch, I felt led to start a ministry to moms. I prayed for the Lord to tell me whom He wanted me to enlist to help, and He literally placed Lisa's beautiful face in front of me.

When our daughter and son accepted Christ, Lisa taught the new Christians class at our church. Lisa was passionate about teaching my children what it meant to be Christians, but more than this, she taught us how critical it is for parents to teach their children to pursue Christ and provide opportunities for them to own their faith personally. Lisa exemplified this and modeled how to be a successful parent through her own journey.

Many years ago, I committed to taking time off of work once a week to attend Lisa's very first parenting Bible study at church. Although my children were already in their teen years, I was hungry to learn how to be effective in my journey as a mom. We were experiencing a little too much "free spirit' in one of our children. I believe this class was a pivotal point in my parenting; it kept us on course with our children, and for that, I am ever so grateful.

Lisa is a parenting mentor; I call her an expert and she corrects me every time, insisting she is not. She has been the parenting mentor for our SkyMoms ministry for nine years. Through Sky Ranch alone, she has ministered to thousands of moms as a keynote speaker and blogger. Lisa has provided endless encouragement to moms as the heart of the home. She has pointed us to Christ for strength and wisdom in the journey, and her book will do the same for you. Her wit and wisdom will captivate you.

Maybe she is not an expert after all, but you could've fooled me. Let's just say, she has been a great role model and an inspiration to so many moms, including me. Lisa will surely encourage you to be all God created you to be!

—Linda S. Paulk
President/CEO
Sky Ranch Christian Camps

Introduction

The Hebrew word *Torah* means "law," especially "instruction for living or "to point by instruction" and comes from the root word *Yareh*, an archery term, meaning "to hit the mark."

The Hebrew word for "sin" is *chatta'ah* (from *chata*, first mentioned in Geneses 4:7), also an archery term meaning "to miss the mark."

June 11, 2003
Here I am crying again. What is going on? Why can't I just

deal with the fact that my eldest daughter is a teenager and doesn't need me like she used to? I know that what she is doing is supposed to happen, but I feel so empty on the inside. I ran into Michelle today, and she said she is so excited about the parenting teens Bible study! I smiled and said, "Awesome! Tell your friends! It's going to be great!" As I walked away I thought, "What am I doing? I'm not emotionally equipped to lead this study. I am struggling to deal with it myself! I don't want her to grow up. I don't want her to talk to her friends and not to me. Why is it that the one thing I feel I am halfway good at is going by so quickly?" God, why do things have to change?

> When I look into her eyes, I see an eighteen-month-old toddler singing, "I'm in the Lord's Army," while her daddy videos and I look on so proudly. Lord, show me how to do this. I am breaking inside, and I need You to show me how to do this.

I grew up in a Christian home with two parents who loved the Lord. We went to church every week, several times a week. We were the typical Baptist family. There was so much right about my family upbringing. And, as most families go, so much was wrong. Somewhere along the way, we went off course, and my parents split up. I remember that day like it was yesterday. My dad called us into the living room. Stop. That was an unusual thing in itself. My dad never really called us in to meet. Or talk. Or catch up. My dad rarely spoke. So, we knew something was up. When he sat my two sisters and me down, my world turned upside down. I had never really heard my parents argue. I knew there were financial issues because my mother got tense every time my dad pulled the "mandarin orange box" down from the closet where he stored all the bills and sat down at the kitchen table. I can't really stomach mandarin oranges to this day. Knowing now that financial struggles are a leading cause for divorce, I suppose my family fell victim to it even back then. We moved every couple of years so we could pay off debt with the equity in the home. They never really told us why they were divorcing, but I think that played a big part. The official reason my parents gave us for the "D" word was,

"We drifted apart." The weird thing was, my dad continued to live with us indefinitely until he could afford to move out and get his own place. I can still remember the U-Haul sitting in front of our suburban home containing half of our furniture. There were no words for that moment. All I know is everything changed that day. Family changed. Relationships changed. I changed.

Most of the change happening at that time wasn't good. I began second-guessing everything I had ever known or learned—not spiritual things but commitment and love. Family was no longer important to me. For the next three years, I was in *the pit.* If you've been there, you know it's not where you want to be. Because I was raised in a Christian home and accepted Christ as my Savior at a young age, I knew I was in *the pit.* I had the Holy Spirit reminding me on a daily basis that I wasn't listening to or acknowledging Him. But I always felt His presence. Because of that, I am forever grateful to my parents for raising me to know Christ.

In 1981, four years after my parent's divorce, I was attending Stephen F. Austin State University where I met Brad, and we fell in love. Interestingly, Brad and I both were attending College Heights Baptist Church there in Nacogdoches on the main drag in town. A friend in my dorm invited me to this church, and I was open and ready to seek the Lord. This is actually where Brad and I met, and we became fast friends and eventually fell in love. I would say those years sealed my faith. I was finally ready to come out of *the pit* I had been living in and be who God called me to be. College Heights brought me the community I longed for. I learned and grew and was discipled in God's Word on a weekly basis. Brad and I both matured so much in our relationship with Christ during those pivotal years.

We married in 1986. Our marriage was biblically solid, and we were serving the Lord at Prestonwood Baptist Church. Brad was even privileged to serve as a deacon. In 1989, we had our first of two daughters, Caroline Elizabeth. She was born on August 9, 1989 (8/9/89—easy for any parent [or husband] to remember!). She was the apple of her daddy's eye and the spitting image of him as well. She looked like him, acted like him, and thought like him. I truly only gave birth to this child. Caroline was extremely precocious. She was singing songs and saying complete sentences at eighteen months. We were so proud.

Our second daughter came along in December of 1993. Camryn Noel was my child. She looked and acted like me—a chip off the ol' block! And Brad was smitten. We had two daughters. Now we were doubly blessed and doubly proud.

I remember feeding Caroline while we were still in the hospital a day or so after she was born and thinking to myself, "What just happened? Now what?" If you're a mom, you know this feeling. I have this child totally dependent on me, and I have no clue what to do with her. The precious angel who is crying needs me but, in the words of Prissy from *Gone with the Wind,* "I don't know nothin' 'bout birthin' babies!!" That was me. What just happened? I felt totally inadequate that day—truly helpless.

Fast-forward almost fourteen years to my journal entry. What just happened? My daughter is almost fourteen years old. That's how fast it goes. Baby to teen in a split second, and I'm not happy about it. Of course, I'm happy for her, just not happy for me. That day was the beginning of a journey that I would have never seen coming in a million years. I had no idea that God would call me into parent ministry, mom ministry to be exact. I truly feel God has given me a word to moms about raising children based on *His* Word. I'm not a perfect parent by any means and cringe when people use the word "parenting expert." How can anyone be an expert at something a hormonal fifteen-year-old girl (or boy!) is doing? It's not possible. No,

I'm not an expert at anything, really. But I do believe God has given me some thoughts about parenting with intentionality and purpose according to His plan.

So, that's the basis of this book! God has given me a ministry to moms and a word about parenting children based on intentionality and His Word. In obedience, I am now putting those words to paper in the form of this book, *Raising Sinners.* After almost twelve years of speaking about raising our little sinners (yes, sinners saved by grace), I am now writing this book to help you during your parenting journey. It has been a joyful journey for me; that's for sure! And I know it can be for you, too.

CHAPTER 1

Loving Your Child Too Much

Some time later, God tested Abraham's faith. "Abraham!" God called.

"Yes," he replied. "Here I am."

"Take your son, your only son—yes, Isaac, whom you love so much—and go to the land of Moriah. Go and sacrifice him as a burnt offering on one of the mountains, which I will show you."

The next morning Abraham got up early. He saddled his donkey and took two of his servants with him, along with his son, Isaac. Then he chopped wood for a fire for a burnt offering and set out for the place God had told him about. On the third day of their journey, Abraham looked up and saw the place in the distance. "Stay here with the donkey," Abraham told the servants. "The boy and I will travel a little farther. We will worship there, and then we will come right back."

So Abraham placed the wood for the burnt offering on Isaac's shoulders, while he himself carried the fire and the knife. As the two of them walked on together,

Isaac turned to Abraham and said, "Father?"
"Yes, my son?" Abraham replied.
"We have the fire and the wood," the boy said, "but where is the sheep for the burnt offering?"
"God will provide a sheep for the burnt offering, my son," Abraham answered. And they both walked on together.

When they arrived at the place where God had told him to go, Abraham built an altar and arranged the wood on it. Then he tied his son, Isaac, and laid him on the altar on top of the wood. And Abraham picked up the knife to kill his son as a sacrifice. At that moment the angel of the Lord called to him from heaven, "Abraham! Abraham!"

"Yes," Abraham replied. "Here I am!"
"Don't lay a hand on the boy!" the angel said. "Do not hurt him in any way, for now I know that you truly fear God. You have not withheld from me even your son, your only son."
Then Abraham looked up and saw a ram caught by its horns in a thicket. So he took the ram and sacrificed it as a burnt offering in place of his son. Abraham named the place Yahweh-Yireh (which means "the Lord will provide"). To this day, people still use that name as a proverb: "On the mountain of the Lord it will be provided."

Then the angel of the Lord called again to Abraham from heaven. "This is what the Lord

says: Because you have obeyed me and have not withheld even your son, your only son, I swear by my own name that I will certainly bless you. I will multiply your descendants beyond number, like the stars in the sky and the sand on the seashore. Your descendants will conquer the cities of their enemies. And through your descendants all the nations of the earth will be blessed—all because you have obeyed me."
Then they returned to the servants and traveled back to Beersheba, where Abraham continued to live. (Genesis 22:1–19)

Watching Abraham's faith unfold as he offered up his precious son, Isaac, is a gut-wrenching story. What resonates with me each time I read this passage is that Abraham's love for God far surpassed his love for his boy. And we know he loved his boy, Isaac. He adored him. But, he *loved God more*.

I love the quote by Helen Keller's teacher, Anne, to her mother, in the book, *The Miracle Worker,* "I don't think Helen's worst handicap is her deafness or blindness. I think it's your love." How many times do we act out of love for our children only to handicap them? It's as though we think they truly are ours. God created them in His image, and we get the privilege and honor of raising them, but they are still His. But, we hold on to them with a vice-like grip, even holding God at bay at times in hopes of keeping them close. I suggest there are several ways we love our kids too much. Oh, I guess there are more, but let's focus on three:

Controlling Them Like They Are Our Own

Say this. Do this. Don't say this. Don't do this. Babies require our care 24/7. We all agree with that. And then toddlers really need us to watch them and protect them from themselves. They are into everything while walking, crawling, climbing, and pulling up. We have to safeguard our homes during those toddler years so they will get into the least amount of trouble. Preschool comes quickly, and then elementary school is here before we know it. During the elementary years, I like to think of Mom as still in the game—controlling and making decisions, even though we are not with our child all day, every day. Our children are still dependent through elementary school. They still need us watching over them like a hawk for the most part. But then the middle school years happen upon us. Where did the time go? He or she is no longer a baby but a *preteen*.

AAAGHHHHHH!!!!! These are the years where we take a few steps back. We open the gate a little—not a lot but a little—allowing them to make a few decisions that reflect their heart, and then letting them learn from those decisions. We do *not* call the teacher every day. We allow them to get to know friends outside of the safe zone of friends we know. These middle school years are truly great years to test the waters for what lies ahead. You can continue to open the gate wider as they enter into high school if they've been proven trustworthy during the middle school years.

However, if we continue to control in the middle school years as we did in elementary, our children don't learn to reason, think, compare, or discern as they should on their own. If we remain the puppet master too long, when they are old enough to physically and legally live on their own, they won't know how to make good decisions themselves. They'll just go along with whoever makes a decision, and usually it's not in their best interest.

Overcommitment

I remember a dad we knew when our children were young who was excited beyond anything to get *his boy* into soccer because he was a soccer player in high school, and he couldn't wait to coach him and teach him *his ways!* That poor little guy had no choice but to play soccer. And actually, as I remember it, he really liked it. However, when they started to see that he had *potential* (the word every parent longs to hear about their offspring), they signed him up for every skills class known to man—several select teams, travel teams, and school teams! You can imagine that poor boy had no life outside of soccer, and when his mom sat down and asked "How did this happen?" her only response could and should have been, "*We did this*!" Four-year-olds don't over commit themselves; parents do this.

Activities and learning are awesome! However, balance in everything is so important. I know we don't want our kids to miss out on anything. If their friends are involved in an activity or a sport, we want our kids to be in on it, too. But here's the trouble: when our children's activities and crazy lives start to determine *when* we eat, *what* we eat, *when* we sleep, *when* we go to church, *if* we go to church, and the list goes on, then we have essentially given our children leadership of our home. They're the boss. They're in control. And, when an eleven-year-old is in control of a home, he is doomed to fail because eleven-year-olds aren't meant to be in charge of much, let alone a home. We are setting our children up for failure when we allow their lives to take over our home. We must pull back the reigns, take time away, and determine what needs to go when this happens. Overcommitment can lead us down a path we were not looking to go down without our even knowing we are on that road.

Planning Their Future

When I think about planning my children's futures, I have to laugh out loud. If only I could! When you raise independent, self-secure children, planning their futures goes out the window. Whether it's a spouse, college, or career, when we try to make it happen, it typically doesn't. And if it does happen, we pay in the end. The only remedy to this act of love is to allow God room to work in our lives and in the lives of our children.

> *"For I know the plans I have for you," says the Lord. "They are plans for good and not for disaster, to give you a future and a hope." (Jeremiah 29:11)*

In other words, claim Jeremiah 29:11 and let go. God holds their lives in His hands. We have a role and a purpose in our children's lives, but their lives are in His hands. We can put a Longhorn jersey on him the day he leaves the hospital after being born, but he just might not have the DNA to be a Longhorn or an Aggie or a Sooner or a Lumberjack. Well, maybe a Lumberjack.

Let's talk now about practical ways *to not love our child too much.*

Chores

Give them chores at an early age. This brings them into the family fold and teaches them how a family system works. Whether it's making their bed at the age of two and picking up their toys in their room before bedtime, or taking out the trash and clearing the table after dinner when they're a pre-teen, or cleaning up outside after the dog does his business—everyone can help! Even the littlest among us and the oldest, busiest among us needs to help. And Mom, if it isn't done mommy perfect—get over it! A two-year-old isn't going to make her bed mommy perfect. She will when she goes to college but not in your home—*ever*! Accept it! But if she makes it and takes responsibility for her room, then you are on the right track.

We had high school Bible study at our home every Wednesday night when our girls were growing up. So Wednesday was the day the girls got it in gear and cleaned nearly mommy perfect. Laundry was put away. Beds were made. Bathrooms were Lysoled. The upstairs was vacuumed. I called the upstairs their "apartment." This kind of made cleaning fun when it was your apartment. Get creative! Make it fun!

RSVP

If your child is old enough to talk on the phone, have him start RSVPing himself. This teaches him responsibility and how to take initiative. It's just right to respond to someone, and let them know you are coming! Geez!

Take Care of Business

Even elementary school children can and should deliver their own notes to a teacher, ask questions, and turn in their school work. When your child makes a grade they're not proud of, have them ask the teacher what they could have done differently. Many moms go into mom mode way too soon. Use these trials as teaching opportunities to give your child room to ask, think, and show initiative. You'll know when you need to get involved.

Filling Out Forms

I *loved* letting our girls write their names down on the waiting room list at the doctor's office. If it was their appointment, they wrote their name down (if they could!). When they were old enough to write their name/address/birth date down on the forms, I allowed them to do this, as well. Mom, just because we can do it better doesn't mean we need to do it. It's okay. Pressure off.

Show Respect

I think the best way to teach respect is to show respect. Sometimes parents don't feel the need to show their children respect. "He's a kid! He needs to show *me* respect!" Well, that's true, but modeling how to be respectful is the best teacher of respect. For instance, take cell phones. (Chapter 1 and we're already talking about cell phones—sigh.) When my girls were growing up, I had a cell phone. They did, too, at different intervals. It broke my heart when I would see a mom on her cell phone in the car pool line talking, talking, talking, and then it was her child's turn to get in the car! Imagine the scenario: she's been away from her child all day long. Her child is hungry, tired, possibly discouraged, didn't perform well on a test, or maybe has incredible news to share with Mom! The child gets in the car, and all she hears is "blah, blah, blah," Mom talking on her cell phone. Mom continues to talk on her cell phone as she exits the school parking lot. This isn't respect. This is oblivion. The sad part is, when her child is old enough to reciprocate, she most likely will.

Don't Make Excuses

If your child messes up, accept it and move on. We spend more time making excuses for our children than we do teaching them how to do it differently next time. Why? Because we feel their actions are a reflection of us and not their own sinful nature. When we make excuses for our kids, we are keeping God at bay and not allowing Him to work on their hearts. Sin is sin. Your child is a sinner. You are raising a sinner. Teach them the ways of the Lord. There are no more excuses.

Spend One-On-One Time with Your Children

Have fun with your kiddos one-on-one! Let them know how special they are! Make memories, plan meaningful conversations, and just be together. And while I'm at it, spend one-on-one time with your spouse, too! (Dating is not just for courtship!)

Pray

Pray for your children. You are going to read this point throughout this book *a lot*—a whole lot. And let them know you're praying for them. Mom, if you aren't praying for your children, who is? A grandparent? Teacher? It is our high privilege to pray for our kids. Taking the time daily to lift them to the Lord by name is an honor and privilege we can't afford to dismiss. I would often text my girls a Scripture and the words, "I'm praying for you now! Anything in particular I can pray for?" or "How can I pray for you today?" These words empower our kids to know someone is interceding for them. I need to know this, and my kids need to know this.

When Caroline was living in Los Angeles, I remember distinctly the day she called me and said, "Mom, I need you to pray for me. I don't want you to worry or go into the fetal position somewhere; I just need you to pray to Jesus for me. Can you do that?"

Ummm, yeah. I think I can. I think I can. Of course, I can!

Ending this chapter with this topic is so appropriate. True love is submitting to the Father. If we truly love our children, we'll give them back to the Lord in prayer, in our actions, and in our devotion to Him. It really does take parenting full circle.

Chapter 2

The Supermom Syndrome

No one goes into parenting with the attitude of "Well, I'll do my best, but I can't make any guarantees." No! We all want to be good parents. Our kids are our trophies, right? We all want trophies to prove we're the best! Oh dear. Sad but true. I was watching the news recently, and a story ran about this exact thing. In fact, there's a reality show on TV called *Trophy Kids*. Sports parents gone wild is what the title should be. I spoke on the topic of "*Supermom Syndrome*" this year, and a friend sent me a text after she heard me speak, letting me know that it really is a "thing." It really is an epidemic. I said, "Duh!" She then sent me a picture of a counseling center with groups available to women who suffer from "The Superwoman Syndrome—Women who feel they must do it all."

So here's the deal: we cannot do it all. And we shouldn't want to do it all as believers in Christ. God never intended for us to do it all. We should always leave room for God to intervene, take control, and do His thing. But our human natural instinct as moms is to *fix it*. We're fixers, and we're really good fixers. And if we can save a child from himself, then we've done our *Supermom* thing well, right?

One of the best feelings in the world is to lay our head down on our pillows at night and feel accomplished. The *big* exhale comes and is followed by that huge sense of accomplishment! You know the feeling, don't you? The lunches are packed. Dinner was delish. The clean underwear is packed away neatly in the chest of drawers. The floors are clean, inbox emptied, bills paid, and the dog fed. Well done, *Supermom*! And then there are the do-over days. The days where we lay our head on our pillows and think, "Man, I need a do-over." Yes, those days!

We all want balance in our lives. And my to-do lists help me gain that desired balance. I love to make to-do lists. The best part of a to-do list is crossing off the to-dos that have been done. Amen? Accomplishment! Yes!

Done! I love how God uses two women in the Bible to speak to this very topic of balance. Luke 10:38–42 tells the story of Jesus entering Martha's home, and Mary immediately sits at His feet while Martha slaves away in the kitchen.

However, right before this story in Luke 10:25–37, Jesus shares an even more poignant lesson. Jesus addresses the heart matters of the lawyer and instructs him on how to live a Christ-centered life. Jesus reminds him that he must "love the Lord your God with all your heart, soul, and mind, and your neighbor as yourself" and illustrates this truth with the parable of the Good Samaritan. Love Me. Serve others. This is how God defines balance. Can you see yourself in either Mary or Martha? Now be honest! Mom, are you sitting at His feet daily? Are you loving God fully? Are you serving others? Therein lies the balance.

Wanting to be a supermom isn't a bad thing. We all want to be super at what we do. It's the "I can conquer the world and make everyone happy and do everything for everyone and please everyone" mentality that isn't possible. It is exhausting just writing that, much less doing it. Being a supermom is one thing. Attempting to be *Supermom* is another. Having balance and resting in the Lord takes practice and planning. It doesn't come naturally. The enemy uses busyness, fear of failure, idolatry, success, and power to immobilize us. The enemy wants you to feel like you *can do it all*. He knows you can't. We lose. And our families lose.

So, how do we find balance, make the main thing the main thing, *and* be a super mom without trying to be *Supermom?* Here are some ideas:

Pray

I know, I know. Here it is again. Pray. Prayer is the key to releasing your children to the Lord on a daily basis. You can't do it all. You can't be with your children 24/7, but God can. So when you lift them up to Him through prayer, you are giving Him permission to work in the hearts and lives of your children. And you are giving yourself permission not to fret or worry or panic or try to fix everything in your child's world. Prayer works. Prayer brings freedom. Be intentional and deliberate and consistent with this every day.

Entrust your children by name to God's capable care daily. Place them at His feet daily. Do your children know you as a praying mom? Or, are they afraid to bring their needs and requests to you because it might freak you out or you'll tell everyone—except Jesus?

I was getting ready to speak at a SkyMoms luncheon several years ago, and Camryn sent me a text. She was a freshman in college at the time, and said she needed some help with Scriptures to send to a friend who needed encouragement. I quickly went to my Bible and started looking up Scriptures and sending them to her for her friend. Later that day, after the luncheon, I checked in on her to ask if her friend received the Scriptures and if they had helped. She said, "Yes, Mom they helped. Actually, it wasn't for a friend. It was for me." Gulp. I had two choices at that point: cry or rejoice. I decided to do both.

Plan

Planning ahead is not my strong suit. I'm just being real. I like to wing it. My family tells me this often. This is not new news. I'm laid back. My husband, on the other hand, well, he's a planner. He plans everything—twice. We are like oil and water. But anyway, "they" say you accomplish 80 percent of what you write down. So going with that theory, let's say we make a to-do list of twenty-two things and accomplish 80 percent. That's 17.6 things we get to cross off our list. That's pretty good. I'll take that as a great accomplishment. So planning ahead is important in life, not just parenting. Planning also helps me not be a crazy lady mom. Suggestion: Take fifteen minutes tonight to plan tomorrow.

Are you a goal setter? We are. We have a Dream Board with all our hopes and dreams for the next ten years. It's fun to dream. We were created to dream. But dreams can become reality *if* you're willing to work at them. Plans put dreams into motion. My family sets goals twice a year: family goals and individual goals. Both are important for growth. We focus on the four areas identified in Luke 2:52 "And Jesus grew in wisdom, stature, and in favor with God and man." Some years we have more success than others, but we *always* are aiming higher, striving to reach our goals.

When Caroline lived in California, one of the biggest blessings was receiving her goals via email one January. Brad and I were both so thankful to not only know "she got it" but she wanted us to pray along with her for her year. There is an old saying that the best way to get nowhere is to have no goals! Are you getting anywhere? Is your family? Maybe you need to set some goals! (See chapter 8.)

Prepare

Hard work and preparation. Yuck! Who wants to do that? Here's what I mean by prepare. Prepare for setbacks, glitches, and unforeseen chaos. We know it's going to happen, so be prepared. I prepare my week by planning coffees one day a week, lunches (business or casual) one day a week, and one stay-at-home day. I know when your kiddos are young this might not be possible, but I *loved* being home one day a week without meetings, coffees, practices, and so on. I just devoted my day to our home and family. That was my day to refuel. But I quickly learned that the only way I could accomplish this day at home required that I planned and prepared for it. I literally had to schedule it in on my calendar. Otherwise, it would never just happen. Preparation builds upon planning.

Here's my favorite part about preparing for setbacks. I like to be free to allow the Holy Spirit to move and guide me. If I'm overcommitted, then I might not recognize that still, small voice leading me to take a dinner to a neighbor, call a sick friend, or visit someone in the hospital. I really do want to do those things, but time doesn't allow it if I'm not prepared. If you're like me, you have a mental list of people you'd like to connect with if only time allowed. Preparing to go off script allows you time to be spontaneous and guided by the Spirit.

When I was in my early thirties, I wanted to go deeper in my faith. Our girls were young, and I really wanted to teach them the ways of the Lord by modeling His ways. So I began a prayer journey. I prayed about everything: what we ate, what we wore, and where we went—everything. One day we were on the way to visit my grandfather at his nursing home in Richardson, and I felt the Spirit of the Lord leading me in a different direction. It was as though the car was being driven by someone else. I went with it. We were driving down a street I had never driven. I was going with it. Down the street,

I saw a man walking with a red Texas Rangers cap on. My grandfather was a devout Rangers fan. As we drove closer to the man walking down the street, I realized it was indeed my grandfather! Nervous, anxious, afraid, I got out of the car and asked him to get in. He obliged, and we took him back to his facility—a mile and a half away! He had escaped and was heading back to Paris, Texas where he was from.

I share that story to make this point: had I not gone on that pursuit to know God more, to sit at his feet, and trust Him with the little things (food, clothes, visits), I would have missed out on this opportunity to see Him work and *use me*. If we don't *know* the Spirit's still, soft voice, we won't recognize it. If we don't pray and communicate with God, we might miss Him talking to us. This is a divine union. Preparing ahead and leaving room for the Holy Spirit to work and lead in our lives allows us to not only grow spiritually but to show our children how God works when we make ourselves available to Him.

Pull Over

When we speed down the highway, what may or may not happen? We might get away with it, right? Or, we may see flashing red lights behind us telling us we got caught! If we see those lights, do we have more than one option? Can we say, "Oh gosh he caught me, but he'll certainly catch another gal speeding, so I'll just keep going." That's not an option, is it? We *must pull over*, or we'll be on the ten o'clock news!

For moms, pulling over is hard. Taking time for oneself is something that just doesn't come naturally. We are doers. So whether it's a book club or night out on the town or a birthday celebration with friends, mani/pedi, weekend getaway, or *whatever*, we must pull over occasionally. To be a super mom, we must allow ourselves time to be refreshed and renewed by spending quiet time with the Lord, resting and quieting our minds. Enjoy life! Even Jesus took time away to be refreshed and renewed (Mark 6:31). Don't get a case of mom guilt. It's a real thing. Mom guilt is rampant. You are worth it! Your family is worth it! And your family will benefit from it! *Pull over*!

Pledge

Okay, so now you get to take the *pledge*. Stand up. Put your hand up in the air like you just don't care. (hehe) Repeat after me.

I am *not Supermom*.
I am a *super mom* but I am not *Supermom*.
I don't even like the *Supermoms* I know!
I know God created me for a relationship with Himself, and I will find my identity in *who* I am in Christ, not who the world says I should be.
I can't do it all, and I don't really want to do it all.
Lord, help me to pray, plan, prepare, and pull over.
Because *Supermom* is a myth. And I'm the *mythbuster*.

Amen. Hallelujah. Class dismissed.

Chapter 3

A Mother's Short Prayer

Dear Lord,
Help me to be the person I expect my kids to be.
Amen.

This may be the shortest prayer ever written. Is it full of truth? Absolutely!

As moms, we expect *so much* out of our children. And we should. Teaching them to shoot for the stars and all that is important. However, in my opinion, we are unwilling to do, speak and be much of what we want to see in our children.

> *Students are not greater than their teacher. But the student who is fully trained will become like the teacher. (Luke 6:40)*

As moms, we are teaching *all day long*. We teach what we eat, what we drink, how we talk, when we talk, what we watch, what we don't watch, how we serve, who we serve, what we read, and the list goes on and on. We are constantly teaching our children as we model for them how to do life. We just forget, in the day-to-day motions of life, that little eyes are watching and little ears are listening. We never get a day off from teaching, unfortunately—no summer break! And we can't punch out.

If we want to see a certain behavior in our children, we have to be willing to model it. We have to be willing to learn new things if we want our children to learn what they need to know. We are *all* a work in progress. Never think it's too late to be the person you want your children to be. Never. And *never* think that, just because you've done it this way for years, it's too late to quit or modify your behavior.

When Caroline was in high school and Camryn was in middle school, I had succumbed to letting them watch a particular reality show. I didn't feel good about it at all. But, "everyone was watching it." Yeah, right. Anyway, one day I really felt the Holy Spirit telling me to "let it go." Not the bad feeling—the show. Let the show go. In other words, delete it from the DVR. Yes you guessed it. There was flailing and gnashing of teeth, but they got over it. And I was able to explain to them that just because we had been watching for months, didn't make it right. We needed to make a change.

It's okay to change, and it's okay to admit to your kiddos that you made a mistake in allowing it in the first place. I've had to apologize to my kids many times as well as ask for their forgiveness. And in doing so, I was given the opportunity to model these biblical actions for them. At first, they were very surprised by my apologies and requests for forgiveness. But they were beautiful teachable and modeling moments! Their tender responses of "It's okay, Mom" always blessed me, too. We need to understand that we are all a work in progress. Sometimes I think I need that yellow tape with the words "Under Construction" wrapped all around me! God's work in me will *never* be done on this side of Heaven, and I am okay with that! I want my girls to understand that we *all* have much refining to do to look more like Jesus, no matter our age! No one expects you to be perfect in this parenting thing, but God does expect us to strive for excellence as we model life for our children.

If you tend to be gossipy and have noticed the same characteristic in your child, then *stop*. This is definitely *not* what you want to model for your children. Pray for self-control to *not* be a gossip. Pray that God will strengthen you to quit. God's Word speaks specifically to the power of the tongue to bring life or death and the sin of gossip. Spend a few minutes in the Book of Proverbs to discover for yourself how God really feels about gossip. By spending time daily in God's Word, you will begin to fill your mind with the things that are important to Him. This will raise your level of awareness and sensitivity to know when a situation to engage in gossip is coming, and then you can *know* you've been equipped by God to not gossip! Plan *now* to gossip *no more*! Arm yourself with God's word for self-control. Now these are the things you want to model for those young ones, right?

"Remember, your actions speak louder than your words!" Did you ever hear these words growing up? I sure did! Or how about this one, "More is caught than taught!" Or maybe this one, "Do as I say *not* as I do!" As a young mom,

I quickly learned the truth and importance of these sayings, and I had to make a major decision: was I going to be the type of parent who *told* my children what to do and how to act, or was I going to be the type of parent who lived out and *modeled* the actions and behaviors I wanted my children to duplicate?

I remember when I taught the parenting class for the first time. We invited moms to "launch" the class with us, and they invited their friends. One particular day, I taught on this subject. A mom, who was a friend of a friend, stopped me on the way out of class that day. I'll never forget her statement and concern. She said, "The light just came on for me. I do not want my daughter to be an underage drinker. I want her to make good decisions with regards to alcohol because

I have not. When I go to dinner and drink a few glasses of wine then get in the car and drive home, how does that look to her? Am I modeling the right behavior to her? I don't think so. It just dawned on me that I need to abstain from alcohol while I'm parenting her through these years so that I can set the right example."

Is this easy? No. Is this possible? *Yes*. This mom got it! Each of us as parents must determine in our hearts and in our minds who we want to be and who we want our children to be. Will they be what we want them to be simply because we have modeled it for them? Maybe. Maybe not. As they grow and mature, they will still have to resolve in their hearts and in their minds who *they* want to be. You can, however, confidently know that you have given them the opportunity to see, firsthand, what a life lived for Christ, in pursuit of Him, looks like.

I prayed with a mom this past Sunday to receive Christ. She has a lot of growth ahead of her because she comes from a denomination rooted in works-based salvation. She kept saying to me, "I just don't want to mess this up. I want my kids to see Christ in me, but I'm afraid of disappointing them." It's important for us to realize that we will mess up—in our own strength. But, as believers in Jesus Christ, and as His representative, we are able to *represent him well* because of *Him*, not us.

Who do you want your children to be? There are so many church answers here, but, in reality, we answer that question by our actions. Here are some thoughts:

I want my child to make her faith her own.

I must make daily devotion to Christ a priority so that she sees what that looks like. Church attendance and fellowship with believers is important. Reading God's Word and prayer time is a must. Give her tools to learn and grow in the Word like a Bible "in her language" and a journal for notes and thoughts. Seek out role models and discipleship opportunities. Christian camps are also a great tool.

I want my child to serve others.

I must be a servant. I need to be praying for opportunities for my family to serve not only our community but each other. Modeling this is important. Having a heart for and toward others is important. My pastor, Dr. Jack Graham, always says, "Never repress a generous impulse." When your heart tells you to give, give. Don't look back. It's the same with service. Family mission opportunities are a great way to serve and teach this incredible quality.

I want my child to be a leader.

Leadership is taught but also learned. Leadership and having an outgoing personality are not the same. Not all leaders are outgoing. So don't think your child can't be a leader if he's shy. He can. Give him opportunities to lead in the family so that he can gain confidence. And, make sure you are leading well. Leadership gets a bad rap because sometimes leaders are bossy. There are so many books on leadership. Get some good ones and share with your family members. John C. Maxwell and Charles Swindoll are two of my favorite authors on this subject.

Well, you get the picture. Expecting our children to be different (i.e., better) than us is not fair. However, it can happen because God is able. I look at it this way: if I try to resemble the person I want my kids to be, then I'm that much further along in my pursuit of representing Jesus Christ with my life to my family and to the world.

Imitate me, as I imitate Christ. (1 Corinthians 11:1)

Chapter 4

Sharing My Past with My Children

Our past scares us, doesn't it? It's hard and scary to think about the days gone by and who we were back then. I guess it really does haunt us some days. Everyone has a past, so we do have that in common. Mine looks one way, and yours looks another, but we all have one.

I love to hear people's stories—where they grew up, how they grew up, and all the other "growin' up" stories. People's stories are interesting. They are all so different but so very similar. Parents, siblings, school—that familiar thread runs through each of our stories. They're so different yet so the same. The questions started coming early-on from moms regarding how or when to share about their past with their kiddos. Heck, I was even nervous about this one! When? How? What? Why?

As we begin looking at this, and as I start to share what God has laid on my heart with regard to this subject, let me share something with you. Recently, I was with some friends having lunch and was asked a very interesting and intriguing question. *If you could have anyone you want join us for lunch, who would it be?* Of course, immediately names like Barbara Bush, Mary, the mother of Jesus, and the like, were mentioned—as well as grandmothers and fathers and other such heroes. I pondered for a few minutes, and without hesitation said, "My seventeen-year-old self." I would love to visit with my seventeen-year-old self and tell her:

> It's going to be okay. You are going to figure this out and move on. God redeems and restores and makes all things (you!) new. You are worthy of His sacrifice. He loves you. He won't ever leave you. You are loved and precious to Him. It's going to be okay.

So without going into all the gory details, my past isn't pretty. It's a past I don't really want to share with my girls. I have, however, shared strategically through the years bits and pieces when it made sense to do so.

Regardless of what your past looks like, you have possibly fretted about how to tell your kids. Or, you dumped on them every sordid detail and wish you hadn't. Alternately, you and your hubby have made a pact in blood not to tell anything—not one item. Don't ask. Don't tell. Mom, I am going to say this with all humility and boldness: the only person who cares about your past is Satan. He cares. Here's why he cares: if he can keep you in your past, then he has you right where he wants you. If he can keep you in bondage, you think you have no influence, and your parenting is in fear.

Your kids don't really care about your past. They are much more consumed with their own existence. Haven't you figured that out by now? It's their world, and you are just passing through. I'm sorry, but it's true. All your kids care about is who you are today. If you are living your life in freedom and in grace, you are much more approachable, and you are a powerful woman of influence.

Moms I've spoken with through the years are typically one of two types of moms: there is the mom who never got a detention or a mark for bad behavior, and the only discipline she received in high school was a note sent home for chewing gum. Were you that mom? I hate you! No, just kidding. Then we have the mom who was, well, opposite of Mom number 1. 'Nuff said.

Both moms have hesitations about talking with their kiddos about their past. Mom number one doesn't want her kids to feel isolated from her or unrelatable if they do stumble and fall: *I don't want them to feel like I was perfect or that they will let me down if they get a detention or get caught cheating on a test. We all make mistakes. I want them to know I wasn't perfect. I just didn't want to get in trouble.* And, Mom number two is thinking: *I'll never tell my full story in fear they will look at my life* now *and think I made it through okay, so they will, too.* Do you get the picture? It really doesn't matter what your past looks like; there is fear and trepidation in sharing it.

Here's the picture God gave me after weeks of prayer on this subject:

The Holiness of God. He Is Perfect

Mom # 1—Almost Perfect, But Alas, Not

Mom #2—A Hot Mess

As we look at the illustration above, who falls short of God's holiness and perfection? That's right. Both moms. We all fall short. Sin is sin. We all fall short (Romans 3:23).

So, as we look at the "how to's" of talking with your children about your past, it's important to realize that *all* of us are sinners. All of us have sinned. There is no perfect mom. We can look at our past and think great thoughts, or we can look and think disaster. But at the end of the day, it all looks the same to our God. We all need Him. We all need what He did for us on the cross. We have no hope without Him.

The victory is yours today. You have overcome. Leave your past in the past. You have been forgiven in Jesus' name. He has forgotten your past. Yes, you might still be suffering consequences from choices you made because God is a just God. But you can live in victory. All that your kids need to know is you are the woman you are *today* because of the freedom and forgiveness you have in Jesus Christ. Your testimony can be shared at appropriate times in your child's life.

Caroline and Camryn still don't know some of the details of my past. They know my life looked a lot different than theirs, and they know many things were the same. They know the person

I am today is real and authentic, and the joy of the Lord is my strength. What more do they need to know? We have raised them to love the Lord.

So, with Jesus as the focal point, we move on. In teaching our children and using our testimony as strategically as possible, we teach our children that their goal and our goal for them is to be like Christ. He is holy and perfect (1 Peter 1:16), and we need Him in our daily lives to guide us and shape us. The Holy Spirit should be our guide. Mom and Dad are just teachers and mentors in the process. We are not perfect. We make mistakes. So as we look unto Jesus, we find perfection and how things should be.

As we teach our children, here are some ideas for talking to them about your past:

• Remind them you do have experiences that have shaped your life, *but* God is awesome! You have been forgiven, even though you have suffered consequences from those decisions.

• Let them know that while you are still parenting them, you won't be going into details about your past experiences. You'll share bits and pieces through the years when the situation is right, but your goal as a parent is to make Jesus' life and holiness the focus, not your life. You don't want to be the focus. You did many things right (Praise God!), and you did many things wrong!

• Remind them that you were responsible for the choices you made. They will be responsible for the choices they make. With Christ, you can stand strong. Make Him your best friend.

- Your children need to be reminded that you grew up in a different time and culture. Quite possibly your family situation was different (i.e., divorced parents, non-Christian parents, etc.).

- Wrap up the discussion with something like this: "When you are grown, one day, I promise, we will grab a cup of hot chocolate, cuddle up on the couch, and I will tell you my story. But until then, please understand that you will have many hard choices to make along the way. God is always with you. I can only be with you at times. He never leaves you. Trust in Him with your whole heart. He will give you the strength you need. Hopefully, my life experiences and the things that have shaped me will help you, too. I will do my best to encourage you and help you along the way."

Mom, pray today that God will walk with you through this battle of the past. Who you are *today* is forgiven. Have you asked Jesus Christ to save you from your sins past, present, and future? Have you called on the name of the Savior, Jesus Christ, who died on the cross for the sins of the world? We have no hope without Him! Make Him Lord of your life today. He paid it all. He knows your past. He came for your past to be forgotten and for you to live in victory. Praise Him today! King of Glory! Lord of All!

And because you belong to him, the power of the life-giving

Spirit has freed you from the power of sin that leads to death. (Romans 8:2)

Chapter 5

Who's in Charge? Me or My Child?

Have you ever asked yourself this question? I have. Who's in charge here? Me or her? Her or me? We can lose ground quickly if we don't claim our turf and keep it. Parenting is a 24/7 job! In the early years we are proactively parenting. What I mean is we are "in the game" and not going to the sidelines. If you've parented a child for more than five minutes, you know it's exhausting and all consuming. But the early years are particularly "hands on."

Proactive parenting means setting boundaries and goals while establishing the role, identity, and character of the family. This is *who* we are, *what* we do, and *who* we will become. Doing this with confidence is key. So as parents we must establish the boundaries, goals, and who we are as a team in order to effectively and proactively parent. We must have a game plan or strategy ready to be implemented to be both proactive and successful. I remember dropping the girls off at friends' houses and quoting, as they exited the car, "Represent your family well," with smiles and fingers crossed. I wanted them to remember that they were not only representing themselves, but the entire Clark clan and their Heavenly Father. It's not about them—it's about all of us. We are a team. We are family. We are God's representatives!

Confident parents realize they *are the parent.* Repeat after me, *"I am the parent."* Again, but louder. *"I am the parent."* See, that wasn't that hard, was it? This gets especially hard the older our children get and when we want to be their buddy, friend, and confidante. There certainly is a wonderful season ahead in which we can be our children's friend! But it is *not* the primary goal in the active parenting years of our young children. God has clearly defined our responsibility as parents in His Word:

> So commit yourselves wholeheartedly to these words of mine. Tie them to your hands and wear them

> on your forehead as reminders. Teach them to your children. Talk about them when you are at home and when you are on the road, when you are going to bed and when you are getting up. Write them on the doorposts of your house and on your gates, so that as long as the sky remains above the earth, you and your children may flourish in the land the LORD swore to give your ancestors. (Deuteronomy 11:18–21)

Confident parents also realize it's never too late to change. Never. God gives us a new day every day. If you are not at peace about something that happened yesterday, then change it today.

Confident parents never give up. Ever. We just don't quit on our kids.

We fight for them. We fight for our family. Even in the hardest of situations, we keep going. You might go through a situation in the future that seems impossible, and quitting will seem like an option. Don't quit. In this ever-changing world that our children are growing up in, they need to know that we will *never* give up on them—*ever*! Just like God never gives up on us.

> But now, O Jacob, listen to the Lord who created you. O Israel, the one who formed you says, "Do not be afraid, for I have ransomed you. I have called you by name, you are mine. When you go through deep waters, I will be with you. When you go through rivers of difficulty, you will not drown. When you walk through the

> fire of oppression, you will not be burned up; the flames will not consume you. For I am the Lord, your God, the Holy One of Israel, your Savior." (Isaiah 43:1–3a)

Confident parents live an authentic life. I never want my kids to think I'm a fake. I want to be the same person at home, at their school, at church, and at work. Our children see through falsehood. Saying one thing and doing another breeds falsehood. If I'm consistent in my walk with the Lord in every area of my life, they will see it and begin to trust my counsel. And they'll see that it's possible to live a godly life in this fallen world.

If you are starting to feel your family is getting out of control or chaotic, and if you're tired of the "crazy family" syndrome, try these things:

Rank Activities—List everything your kiddos do on a piece of paper then start to rank them 1–10, or 20 (yikes!). Once you've ranked the activities from non-negotiables (church, Awana, etc.) to paint-by-numbers club, choose the ones at the top you want to keep; then *stop* the others. Just stop. Gain control of your family again by saying "No!" to the things that are of less importance or significance and aren't a priority for your family.

Family Traditions—Do you have them? If I were to ask your children what yours were, would they know? Family traditions aren't just for holidays! Sunday night game night, breakfast for dinner, and Saturday morning pancakes, are all examples of fun, family traditions to define your family.

Chores—One is never too young for chores. Chore charts can work, but they have to be used. Children who are given chores feel more a part of the family system and feel like they are contributing to the "well-oiled machine" called family.

Car Rules—This should be obvious, but unfortunately it's not. When your children are in the car, interact with them! Don't be on the phone! And expect the same courtesies from your children. You have a captive audience in the car, so use that time to visit, catch up, teach, or worship. Car time is great family time.

Limit Volunteering—There is plenty of time to overcommit yourself once your children are older. Trust me. Limit your volunteering. Many moms get crazy and feel out of control when *they* are the ones who signed themselves up for everything. Set your own priorities!

Pray—When was the last time you told your child you prayed for him? Or when was the last time you prayed together as a family? Maybe this is a part of who you are as a family. For many it is not. You will find strength and confidence to parent your children the way God has called us to parent them through prayer. Have you shared God's telephone number with your children? What? You don't know God's telephone number? It's Jeremiah 33:3. Call Him today.

Ask me and I will tell you remarkable secrets you do not know about things to come. (Jeremiah 33:3)

Chapter 6

Mom Cops

First, let me define Mom Cops—def. (noun)—*Moms who think it is their sole mission in this life to "police and report" all actions of their friends' kids and their kids' friends.*

Do you know any Mom Cops? More importantly, are you one? (Don't admit it!)

A few years ago, my husband and I went to the movies with another couple. The show we wanted to see was sold out, and we opted for another one—a comedy. We saw *Paul Blart:*

Mall Cop. My husband would tell you he didn't think it was a comedy at all. He thought it was a waste of his twenty-five bucks! I thought it was pretty cute. A mall cop on his Segway, strolling through the mall at a half mile per hour! Pretty funny!

It made me think of moms in mini-vans cruising through neighborhoods, waiting for unsuspecting troublemaker preteens with issues. Look out! She's out to get you! If you've ever had a conversation with a Mom Cop, then you know exactly what I'm talking about. I have had more than one face-to-face with one of these moms, and I don't care if I ever have another one. I remember one instance when a mom called me because she *heard* my daughter was planning on going to a movie with a group of kids, and she didn't feel like the group or the movie was appropriate. Well, as is most often the case, she *heard* wrong. Then there was the time a mom let me know that our family portrait would have been "Perfect, if your daughter's shorts weren't so short!" Thanks, Mom! I needed that!

You see, most often, when Mom Cops deliver their reports, the news is biting, and it stings. Then the relationship is awkward and, many times, fizzles out. Proverbs talks about Mom Cops with agendas:

> Blessings accrue on a good and honest life, but the mouth of the wicked is a dark cave of abuse. A good and honest life is a blessed memorial; a wicked life leaves a rotten stench. A wise heart takes orders; an empty head will come unglued. Honesty

> lives confident and carefree, but shifty is sure to be exposed. An evasive eye is a sign of trouble ahead, but an open, face-to-face meeting results in peace. The mouth of a good person is a deep, life-giving well, but the mouth of the wicked is a dark cave of abuse. Hatred starts fights, but love pulls a quilt over the bickering. You'll find wisdom on the lips of a person of insight, but the shortsighted needs a slap in the face. The wise accumulate knowledge—a true treasure; know-it-alls talk too much—a sheer waste. (Proverbs 10:6–14 MSG)

Many times we get our badge out and slap it on for reasons that are anything but godly or protective. Think about this when you feel it's your job to call a mom or dad about their child: Is their child in a life-threatening situation? Is their child in a life-altering situation? If the answer to either of these questions is "Yes," then by all means, make the call. If the answer is "No," then consider these options:

Pray for wisdom. Don't be foolish or short-sided. Seek the Lord. Don't let your tongue be a source of evil. Remember, we can't take our words back. Even if we speak out of turn, we cannot take back the words that come out of our mouths. Wouldn't you rather be "prayed up" before you approach a parent?

Make sure you don't rush to judgment. Have you validated your story? Many times, the story our children come home with is a half-truth or hearsay. I surely don't want to call a parent with hearsay or gossip.

Consider your reasons for "making a report." Is it to prove a point, to defend your child, or to get back at a family for a prior situation? Is the reason simply hatred or bitterness?

Last, consider your relationship with this person or family. Is this issue worth potentially destroying a friendship or making you appear judgmental and unaccepting?

Speaking from experience, I've never regretted waiting to approach a parent about a particular situation while I was waiting on wisdom from the Lord—never. If it's not a life-threatening, life-altering situation, I wait. I wait for wisdom and direction from God. Opening my mouth immediately most assuredly gets me in trouble. Every. Single. Time.

Social media brings a whole new level of Mom Cop. I can't even go there really. I can't be the social media Mom Cop. And you can't, either. Mom, trust me, your plate is full with your own kiddos and their apps, snaps, chats, pics, texts, tweets, and such. Don't take on the neighbors' kids, too. Just don't. The End. #theend.

CHAPTER 7

MOM is WOW Upside Down

When she speaks she has something
worthwhile to say,
and she always says it kindly.
She keeps an eye on everyone in her
household,
and keeps them all busy and productive.
Her children respect and bless her;
her husband joins in with words
of praise:
"Many women have done wonderful things,
but you've outclassed them all!"
Charm can mislead and beauty soon fades.

The woman to be admired and praised
is the woman who lives in the
Fear-of-God.
Give her everything she deserves!
Festoon her life with praises!
(Proverbs 31:26–31 MSG)

When Camryn was young, I found her crying in her room one day. I asked her, "Cam, why are you crying?" She stumbled around a bit, then through the tears and snot said, "I'm worried I won't be a good mom like you one day." Well then. Let me just say that she hasn't felt that way every day of her life. There were the middle school and preadolescent years. I was, however, blessed, humbled, and overwhelmed by that comment. Wow.

Our role as Mom is never-ending and ever-changing. The one thing it's *not* is boring. We never get a day off. And though our role changes and evolves, our hearts for our children remain completely and forever in sync and in love. *We are lifegivers.* Think back to the day you first gave birth. Or think back to your *Gotcha Day* if you adopted. You became a family that day, and your lives completely changed. You gave life to a family. Immediately, as new moms, we begin to think forward and hope for the day our little one smiles back at us, or starts to sit up or laugh or eat real food or sleep through the night or talk or walk or go to school or—move out.

No just kidding, but really, I was practically cyber bullied one day when a blogger mom of little ones chastised all of us "older moms who have been there done that" for saying things like, "Enjoy your baby, honey, it goes by sooooo quickly." I get it.

You don't want to hear those words when you're running on no sleep, no shower, and no help. When those words come your way, you want to look at the well-meaning older mom and ask her, "Did Satan send you?"

You're *wow* because you're a *life-saver.* Have you ever thought about it? You are practically the fire department, police department, and National Guard all rolled up into one. Every time you take a forgotten lunch up to school, you've saved a life. The kid could have starved to death, by golly! Seriously. Every time you bandage a knee, break up a fight, or give some aspirin, you've saved a life. How about this one, "Mom, I forgot my science project. Can you bring it to school?" Life saved. Bam.

Saving lives is not easy work, but you're up to the task. However, I only saved a life once a semester. So if I saved your life by bringing your lunch to you because you didn't wake up early enough to make it, then you can pretty much guarantee I won't save your life again if you call that same semester. I save a life once a semester. I'm not raising cats.

You are *wow* because you are a *life changer.* You have the power and ability to change a life and a generation. We all want to do it better than our moms. It's a generational contest. Who can do it better? We have so much knowledge at our fingertips. We can do better. We must do better.

Raising children for greatness is the goal. We all want our kids to be great. We have high hopes for them. Unfortunately, raising children for greatness is only one of the goals we have for our kids. There are so many things we want them to pursue, excel at, and become that *great* gets watered down to almost nothing. We lose sight of the changed lives that can be a result of a life sold out to Jesus Christ. It really doesn't matter who or what our children become if they don't meet Jesus. You have the ability to not only introduce your children to Christ but to disciple them and train them to love God with all their heart soul, mind, and strength. And to *serve*. This is a game changer.

Do you have the WOW factor?

Is your home a peaceful place full of redemption, grace, and love?

Do you offer forgiveness balanced with appropriate consequences, teaching your children about life, love, and grace?

Jesus first offered forgiveness to us, and we are commanded to offer it to others, including our children. But many times we expect our children to be perfect. When they sin, we gasp in horror at the idea of raising little sinners. How could this be? When did this happen? Then our children feel like failures and misfits within their own homes. Your children are sinners. Newsflash, you are, too. Offer redemption in your home. Offer forgiveness.

Are you making memories?

Making memories is simple and, most often, in the mundane. Don't wait for an elaborate family vacation to Europe to make a memory. Memories are made every day. Here's a quick reminder to make memories in the everyday life moments: Say it. Show it. See it. Sow it. Don't waste it.

Do you have balance in your life? Are you spending time in prayer and Bible study, having daily devotionals, and participating in community fellowship?

You are *wow*. You are *Mom*. In my opinion, raising children today is harder than it was ten, twenty, or thirty years ago. I believe the pull on their lives is stronger than ever toward evil and self-centeredness. Your home is a refuge. You can change lives through your ministry inside your home. You are *wow*.

> These women have chosen life by bearing children (something only a woman can do, I might add); and they are choosing life every day with every meal they prepare; with every load of dirty clothes they wash; with every trip they make to the grocery store, to school, to the dentist, to piano lessons, to soccer practice, or to the shoe store; with every scraped knee they bandage; with every encouraging word they speak; with every night hour they spend rocking a sick or scared child; with every dispute they arbitrate; with every moment they spend building Legos, coloring, helping with

math problems, reading a Bible story, or listening to a husband or child describe his day; with every moment they spend interceding for the spiritual growth and protection of their family. Day in and day out, they are building a home; they are being life-givers; they are laying a foundation and building a memorial that will outlive them for generations to come; they are honoring their Creator in the greatest possible way. Nancy Leigh DeMoss

Chapter 8

Stay in Your Lane

I'm writing this chapter while in Hollywood, California. First, I love California. It's absolutely exquisitely beautiful. Your plane lands among palm trees and seventy-five degrees of perfection. Caroline lived here for three years, and we made several trips across America to visit her. Glitz. Glamour. Stores I'd dare not ever enter. Coffee shops. Skinny people. Tattoo parlors. Stuff like that.

I think it would be very easy to get caught up in it all here. In fact, living in north Dallas is very similar to Los Angeles. There's a lot of trying to "keep up with the Joneses." Who are the Joneses, anyway? I remember when we had weekly high school Bible studies in our home, and a girl named "Sally" had been coming for several weeks. She was a jeans and t-shirt girl—no pretense; nothing fake. She overheard a few of the girls discussing the fact that they *plan* their "church outfit" the week before. What? She was astonished with the thought of planning out what you would wear to church long before Sunday morning. Girls do this? Oh, yes, they do! Moms do, too.

Back to Hollywood. I'm not going to debate whether it is all real or not. Lots of memories were made here along with great films and amazing entertainment. That is real. Dreams are made here, too. It is definitely a dreamer's paradise. But pretense can be a huge distraction. We see the glitz and glamour, and we want it, whether it is ours to have or not.

Back to our neck of the woods. "Oh, look! That child is on a select soccer team! I want my child on one, too!" "Oh look! She got a new Louis V purse! My daughter needs one, too!" "Oh look! His son is practicing skills on Sunday mornings! I need my son to practice, too!" Our attention is easily diverted to what is happening on the other side of the street. Our game plan changes and suddenly, quite unintentionally, we are off course.

Staying in our lane is hard. We have goals and dreams for our children, and we seriously want the best for them. But as Christian parents, we should want God's best even more. We must stop comparing our child to every other child. Comparison is the thief of joy. You've heard it before. Satan uses comparison to destroy us.

We immediately go from comparing to bearing down on our children with unrealistic expectations because we feel like we are letting them down. Honestly, it is *pushing* our children in the direction we want them to go or excel in rather than guiding them in God's perfect direction. Yes, we want them to succeed, right? How can that be bad? Well, our parenting can quickly move from good to bad when our motivation or "pushing" comes from comparison and feelings of inadequacy rather than God's leading and guidance.

Admitting we are not perfect can help us to stay solidly in our lane.

We will make plenty of mistakes on this journey. I've made my fair share! But we are not alone. Admitting to our children that we are not perfect reminds them, and us, that we are depending on Christ to lead and direct us in this parenting journey.

We can get out of our lane by casting our own insecurities and issues onto our kids. I have had huge dreams for my child because I was an underachiever. My child comes to me one day and says, "Mom, I want to run for an office in the student council. Can you help me make a poster?" Gulp. I immediately revert back to my 4th-grade insecure self, remembering when I ran for student council secretary and didn't win! Then I ask her, "Are you sure?" praying silently that I heard her wrong.

"Our lane" is to be the best cheerleader for our children. "Our lane" is to be the president of their fan club. "Our lane" is not to hold them back or cast fear and insecurity onto them because we don't want them to get hurt or to be disappointed possibly like we were. They will get hurt and disappointed. However, as you and I look back on our own lives, it was those hurts and disappointments that helped shape us into who we are today. We have to pray that God will equip us to cheer on our children rather than cast doubt, undermining their own confidence.

Guardrails help us stay in our lane. As we raise our little sinners, looking at Jesus' example in Luke 2 really gives us a template for areas of focus.

> *And Jesus grew in wisdom and in stature and in favor with God and all the people. (Luke 2:52)*

This scripture points us to four areas of growth for Jesus as a young boy. Early on in my parenting, God gave me a visual for goal setting. I call it a *goal-setting board*. This is a photo of my friend Dianna's board:

Goal Setting Board

When setting goals with our kids, we would first talk about how Jesus grew and give examples of areas of growth. We would ask, for instance, regarding wisdom, "What are some goals you would like to accomplish this year in school? Would you like to make the dean's list? Or "A/B" Honor Roll? Would you like to increase your GPA or be initiated into the National Junior Honor Society? Are you looking to read more books this year or enter a project into the science fair?"

We would set goals with each child on one side of the note card, and on the other side we would include steps to achieve those goals. Then we would proceed with goals for the other three areas: physical (stature), spiritual (in favor with God), and service (in favor with man). We would try *not* to overwhelm our children but would *always* make them a part of the process.

Once each child determined their goals, we began praying over them together as a family and individually. Then in the coming months, it was exciting to see the growth in specific areas and enlightening in other areas if growth was slower. This goal-setting board became a constant visual reminder of our goals and an excellent measuring stick for our progress.

The goal-setting board is also a great visual to see if your child is "off balance" in any particular category. Too many physical goals and one spiritual goal does not make for a well-balanced child. We want to see balance across the board, so we know we are focusing on the right things. The board is also a good visual to create community in your family. When siblings see that their sister really wants to make the soccer team, they can cheer her on.

It dawned on me recently that I don't want to just stay in my lane as a parent. I want to stay in my lane as a child of God. I'm not here to be just a parent or a wife, sister, friend, daughter, or any of the other various hats I wear. Those hats are icing on the cake. Ultimately, I'm here to meet Jesus Christ and be His servant. If I stay in *that lane*, I won't lose my identity when my job descriptions change. Here's what I'm trying to say: If I wake up every day fully devoted to Christ, asking Him, "How can I serve you today?" then my focus is on Him and not on the fact that my kids are grown and living their own lives in other areas of the country.

The details of my day-to-day life will change. That is guaranteed. I'm getting older every day. My kids are grown. My mother lives in a nursing facility. My dad has gone to heaven. My life is changing. But one thing has not and will not change. My Jesus loves me. He lives inside of me, and He gives me purpose and meaning and direction. I am His, He is mine, and that is the lane I want to stay in until I see Him face-to-face in eternity.

> *Obviously, I'm not trying to win the approval of people, but of God. If pleasing people were my goal, I would not be Christ's servant. (Galatians 1:10)*

CHAPTER 9

Flashcards and Other Evil Things

Would you consider yourself smart? Learned? Bright? Intelligent? That's all the words I know for smart. Sorry. If you're *very smart*, you probably put this literary work of art back on the bookshelf nine chapters ago. I have already spoken up and made it very clear that I'm not that smart. There's book smart and street smart. I'm probably somewhat street smart. My kids would say no, but I am.

When your preschooler comes home asking about flashcards, your world crumbles. At least mine did. It is a slow death of, "Where did I go wrong?" and "Why didn't I marry a genius?" mixed with "I'm gonna tell that preschool teacher what she can do with her flashcards."

So, apparently, we needed to work on our numbers and letters. That was the bottom line. I don't know about you, but school was for learning in my day. Home was for fun, food, and fellowship. I missed the memo that our children needed to know everything *before* they went to school. So, we had to get flashcards.

Flashcards were just the beginning of our youngest daughter's school struggles. Academics weren't her thing. She had other things that were her thing, but alas, academics were not one of them. The problem was that school is a big deal. "School is your job!" I so often told my girls. School *is* a big deal in this game of life! One year, the struggle was reading. We got a tutor for reading, and she took off. She actually excelled and became an avid reader. Yea! The next year the struggle was math. Math is evil. Why does one need to *know* math since the invention of a thing called *the calculator*? Can't we all just buy a calculator and be done with it? Nope. We must learn math.

Tears—years of tears: the struggle was real. The good news was that all the other subjects were a piece of cake for her. That was our saving grace. Well, there was the time I asked her, "Are you studying US History this year?" and she proudly responded,

"No, American." Okay, she struggled in other areas, too, but mostly math.

Much ado about nothing, you say? This too will pass, you think smugly? Alert: When it's big in their world, it's big in *your* world. We, as parents, know their seemingly big issues will work out, but *they* don't. So we must meet them where they are and use these struggles as a time to pray, focus, teach, and encourage. If we shove off these moments, we waste precious, limited teachable opportunities.

To the church in Corinth, Paul reminded them what he had been through to proclaim the gospel of Jesus Christ. He had truly been kept alive by God. However, he didn't want to be known as a super hero. He only wanted to be known for "what they can see in my life or hear in my message . . ." (2 Corinthians 12:6).

And then the kicker:

So to keep me from becoming proud, I was given a thorn in my flesh, a messenger from Satan to torment me and keep me from becoming proud. Three different times I begged the Lord to take it away. Each time he said, "My grace is all you need. My power works best in weakness." So now I am glad to boast about my weaknesses, so that the power of Christ can work through me. That's why I take pleasure in my weaknesses, and in the insults, hardships, persecutions, and troubles that I suffer for Christ. For when I am weak, then I am strong. (2 Corinthians 12:7–10)

One of the hardest parts of parenting, I believe, is watching a child struggle. Whether it's socially, mentally, emotionally, academically, physically, it's hard. We want to take their "thorn/splinter" from them, but God has a plan. It's for His glory, not my comfort. Ouch.

Our daughters struggled in different areas. Regardless of the struggle, I was constantly reminding them, "The struggle keeps us on our knees. Without the struggle, we become prideful and self-reliant. We were meant to proclaim the power of the Holy Spirit in our lives, and give Him credit for all. Praise God for the struggle. It keeps us on our knees and dependent on the Father."

Be mindful that God *allowed* Paul's struggle, as He has *allowed* your child, and mine, to struggle. Our struggles do not catch God off guard or off His throne. God reminds us that if He chooses not to remove the struggle, His power and grace are sufficient, and He will see us through it. And, hopefully, we will look more like Christ on the other side of the struggle, which is God's goal.

I was reminded of this very topic yesterday when I received a text from a young mom I disciple. Her text read, "G got in the car today after school and burst into tears. Evidently academic awards had been handed out, and she didn't get one. I'm heartbroken for her." Boy, could I relate to this text. My heart hurt for her. In these moments it's important for us to remind our children *who* they are and *whose* they are. "You're a child of the King of kings and Lord of lords. The earthly awards you receive are nice, and you'll receive plenty of those through the years, trust me. But the awards we pray come your way are the eternal ones. Those accomplishments you achieve in Jesus' name."

Social struggles are just as real as academic and physical struggles. I remember one child coming home, and she didn't get invited to a party. I asked her how she knew she didn't get invited, and she said, "The mom came into the classroom and passed out the invitations to everyone but me." *Oh no, she didn't*! In these painful instances, there's nothing like a soothing mother's voice and prayer that will change a perspective. We need to talk through them, pray through them, and be proactive in our thinking. We are all a work in progress. None of us has arrived. And *the struggle* is a gentle reminder of that.

When your child needs flashcards:

- Pray first. Ask the Lord to meet you and your child in the midst of the struggle.

- Remind your child *who* they are and *whose* they are.

- Discuss ways to serve and represent Christ in his or her day-to-day life. Then celebrate actions of love and service! We would bring out the "Red Celebration Plate" every opportunity we got! There is literally something you could celebrate every day if you want to. You probably don't want to celebrate every day because then it wouldn't be special to celebrate! But you get the picture.

- I loved writing often on the girls' mirror in their vanity area "You're a child of the King of kings and Lord of lords!" If you have boys, you could print scripture affirming who they are in Christ and frame it in their bathroom area.

- Go to the store and get flashcards. Everything will be okay. God's got this, Moms. Everything will be okay.

Update: Our little one who struggled academically in school is preparing to graduate from college with the highest GPA in our family. Thank you, Lord!

CHAPTER 10

My Name is Lisa. I'm an Empty Nester.

August 2015

I took this picture of Camryn and Brad in early summer, knowing what happened a few nights ago would take place this summer. (If you haven't heard, Camryn and Brett got engaged.) When I took this picture, we were out in the backyard enjoying one of our first summer nights together after she returned from her junior year of college. Brad was seeing if she could still hit the can with the BB gun. She could. Before Camryn came home this summer we knew it would be our last with her at home.

I've written a blog in the past, asking moms to count the number of summers they have left with their children at home. When I have asked that question in public, moms literally get teary-eyed counting in their mind. It's hard to imagine not having our kiddos at home during the summer, sleeping in late, lunch on the patio, swimming, wet towels everywhere, late night movies, popcorn, vacations, wet towels, snow cones, Vacation Bible School, tennis lessons, camps, wet towels, and so on.

We are so excited for Brett and Camryn. But this is our last summer with her at home. Our last summer to have a child wake up late and come down all messy haired and ask what's going on. It's the last summer to have a cup of coffee together and compare schedules. She's off to work. Or we lay out by the pool. We might watch an old movie like *Steel Magnolias*, Terms of Endearment, or *Save the Last Dance*. We've loved them all.

It's the last summer for her to come home from college and that feeling of relief. Home! I remember that feeling, albeit very different from her experience, home is home. It's also the last summer for her daddy to empty her car of clothes, books, shoes, guitar, and more shoes.

Life is a garland of moments we drape over the recesses of our minds and hearts. No one can take these moments from us. They are our moments. I treasure these moments. Everything changes for all of us. I'm begging myself to live in the moment. So now we are starting to plan a wedding. Next summer will be *next* summer. *Today* is this summer. I'm going to embrace every last second.

Empty Nesting is a funny thing. It typically occurs when you're going through menopause. That's funny, God–real funny, hilarious actually. No one to yell at but our husbands? GEEEEEZZZZZ.

I don't know what I was expecting during the transition from House of Kids to No House of Kids. But it was actually kind of okay. Should I feel guilty? I love my children; I really do. But I love my husband more. So Empty Nesting has been *all good*.

When Caroline went to college, and then moved to California, we had Camryn still in tow, so it was great. It was a subtle transition from two kids to one, which was no biggie. Then Camryn went to college, and Caroline got married. That. Was. Hard. But we made it; then it was good. Then Caroline and Brent would visit, and Camryn would come home, and life was good again. Then they would all leave. That. Was. Hard. But we made it. Now Camryn is engaged and will graduate soon and get married. That. Will. Be. Hard. But we will make it.

Do you see what happens? It's a little big thing called *life*. It happens, and it is good. In the middle of all these *big life* moments, are the little day-to-day happenings that make the *big life* moments okay. Empty nesting is about adjusting to a new normal and realizing, "Hey, this is good. I kind of like this. They come back periodically. They have lives. They're moving on. We are in love still. Life is good!" That's empty nesting.

But do you see the elephant in the room, Mom? The hubs. He's the elephant in the room. Do you like him? Do you love him? Do you know him? Does he know you? Empty nesting can be a joyous occasion if your relationship with the hubs is all good. Start now making sure it is all good. Today. Start. You will thank me later. I've watched many couples struggle to the point of divorce because they didn't pay attention to their marriage during their parenting years. It's got to be in this order:

1. God
2. Husband
3. Children

That's your priority list. I'm not a marriage counselor, but I know this much: your man has got to be your priority after your relationship with Jesus Christ. Brad and I have tried so hard to keep this in mind with regard to God's best for our marriage. And we've made lots of mistakes. You will, too. But in the end it is worth it. These years are the best years of our lives. Why? We get to see the fruit of our labor. Our kids are grown up and living their lives out in the world representing Jesus Christ. Why would I be sad about this? I am over the moon! And grandkids will be coming soon! What? I cannot wait!

Did you know that marriage counseling is not just for weak individuals? News Flash! Can I just say that many of us need a shot in the arm of counseling or therapy occasionally? It is okay. Seek guidance and a little help if necessary. Your marriage deserves it. Your family deserves it. *Fight for your marriage.*

I'm going to end this chapter with a letter to moms from my soul mate. Brad taught me everything I know about parenting. Well, almost everything. And I'm serious about that. He's the best mom I know.

Dear Moms,

I am not sure if I should be embarrassed, upset, or proud of the title that Lisa has given me as "the best mom I know." I do know and recognize that there is no greater role or title than that of Mom. Our family is blessed to have someone like Lisa take on that role to all of us, including someone like me who needs a little "mothering" along the way. God blessed me as a dad with two precious daughters, but even more so, with a partner in Lisa to make sure they would always have an incredible role model to follow. I am sure I speak for all parents, moms and dads alike, when I say there is no greater joy than being Dad, provider, protector, enforcer, scapegoat, village idiot, and best friend. You see for me, when these little girls came into my life, I was smitten and knew that life for me would never be the same.

Lisa has outlined how different our girls are. One is a mini version of me, while the other is a mini version of Lisa. Of course, they say opposites attract, so it is notable that Lisa's personality is much different from mine. I am a type A personality, driver, with a few friends, sometimes impatient, and I love to hold court to pontificate my thoughts at a moment's notice. Lisa is much more laid back, patient, sweet, caring, with a plethora of friends, hates to compete, and will sit and listen without talking all day long. I know this because I have done the talking, and she has done the listening, for many, many years.

Due to their different personalities, Lisa and I approached parenting Caroline and Camryn differently as well. The basic biblical values were the same, but the approach was much different. For example, Caroline and I could have a very direct, pointed, and aggressive conversation about a subject, and if it did escalate into a disagreement, we had no issue apologizing to one another, and it was over. That approach did not work with Camryn. We had to be much more sensitive and delicate in our approach.

I must say, I was blessed to have an incredible role model in my earthly father. My dad was a great leader who loved God with all of his heart, soul, strength, and mind. I remember putting my dad on a pedestal and wanting to be just like him. He was always the first to lead and the last to take. He was a great man who loved me no matter what I did and no matter what path I chose to take. He took every opportunity to teach, correct, model, and show me how a Godly man loves his wife and loves his children. I will admit, as a sixteen-year-old, those "teaching moments" grew tiresome, but when my daughters came along, I knew that he had prepared me to love and lead my family in the very same manner. Here are the lessons I learned from my father my first twenty-nine years on this earth, and the last twenty-seven years as a parent:

Live what you believe. I love the story in John 14 when the disciples are arguing like children regarding who loves Jesus the most. Jesus responded in 14:21 "Those who accept my commandments and obey them are the ones who love me. And because they love me, my Father will love them. And I will love them and reveal myself to each of them." I believed my kids did not care how much I knew, but what they needed to see was my priorities lived out. I was never perfect, and we all fall under the grace that God brought through the forgiveness he delivered through His son, but I do believe it is important to *show* them how to love God and others and not just *tell* them how to do so.

Build up their self-esteem and teach them to soar like eagles! Isaiah 40:31 says, "But those who trust in the Lord will find new strength. They will soar high on wings like eagles. They will run and not grow weary. They will walk and not faint." I felt it was our job and privilege to raise eagles. As a dad, it is a privilege to know that my kids loved and came to expect "the fly like an eagle lessons and letters." I wanted our kids to know that there would never be any peer pressure so great that could not be overcome if they believed in themselves and knew they were special. They knew they could accomplish anything in life that they set their mind to, and they had the ability to fly like none other. Building self-esteem in your children will return great treasure as they walk through this broken world. Teach your kids to "fly like an eagle!"

Love them unconditionally. This is the agape love that Jesus was talking about when he asked, "Peter do you love (agape) me?" (John 21:15) It is the purest form of love and one I always wanted our kids to experience. I always knew that no matter how successful or unsuccessful I was at school, sports, work, or life, my dad loved me and was always proud of me. That unconditional love is a mighty weapon in the hands of a Christian, young or old, to know there is a place you can go to receive love, encouragement, support, and acceptance, no matter what the world says about you.

Create your home to be a fortress for your kids. There is actually another form of love. The love described by the Greek word *storge* is best understood as family love. It's the kind of easy bond that naturally forms between parents and their children—and sometimes between siblings in the same household. This kind of love is steady and sure. It's love that arrives easily and endures for a lifetime. We always wanted to make our home much more than a structure in which we raised our kids. We wanted our home to be a place our kids wanted to be and always knew was a safe place to be from the outside world.

Discipline—Do not be afraid to be the parent. I believe it goes without saying that if you have read to this point, you know that Lisa and I love our kids very much. We loved them so much we weren't afraid to discipline them when necessary. I remember seeing some of our friends as young parents promising to bring some form of discipline to their children, but that discipline never came. I told these precious gifts from God, our daughters, that I loved them too much to lie to them. If I promised some form of discipline if they disobeyed, they knew I would deliver said discipline. I believe this teaches them the true character of God. Search the scriptures and see that we have an incredible God who loves us, but He is just and does punish sin when those He loves rebel against Him. We weren't trying to be "God like" but wanted the very best for our children. This forced us to discipline them, and not try to be their best friends.

Be intentional. Pursue your children or someone else will! We always made it a point to intentionally pursue our kids. I don't mean putting them up on pedestal and idolizing them or hovering over them constantly, but we made it clear they were our priority. I believe too many parents allow their kids to be overpursued by elements from the outside world including friends, sports teams, music, Hollywood, and so on, while parents go with the flow and just let things happen. If we sit on the sidelines, the world will consume our children. We must be intentional and fight for our families.

Take them to church and show them how to serve. Lisa and I were raised in the local church. We joke that we now live in a small town called Prestonwood. We were married at Prestonwood Baptist Church, our kids were dedicated there, came to know Christ there, and were baptized there. Caroline and Camryn met Brent and Brett at Prestonwood and were married there. God willing, Lisa and I will be buried there as well. Outside of our personal relationship with Jesus, our church has been the single most influential factor in helping us to raise our children. Lisa and I are leaders in the church, and the girls have seen this servant leadership lived out. They are now actively serving in their own churches. There is no greater privilege to see your children grow in their faith and love the church. We are thankful to our church body for helping us raise our sinners.

God bless you all and thanks for the opportunity to share,

—BC

CPSIA information can be obtained
at www.ICGtesting.com
Printed in the USA
BVHW030209030321
601578BV00009B/130